Bitcoin For Beginners

A Simple Guide For Investing In Bitcoin And Other Cryptocurrencies

Introduction

When Bitcoins launched in January 2009, very few people guessed it would become the biggest and most valuable virtual currency in the world. It started from practically nothing with a worth of just $0.0008. But now, Bitcoins are the most expensive virtual currency on the market. At the time of the writing, Bitcoin (or BTC) has a market cap of $175,363,170,760 and is ranked number one of all cryptocurrencies. A single Bitcoin now costs $9,917, making it the largest cryptocurrency on the market (Blockonomi, 2020).

The idea and technology behind Bitcoins were created by Satoshi Nakamoto, whose real identity is still a mystery. From 2009 to the present, Bitcoin has faced its ups and downs, been praised and criticized, with its value fluctuating in-between.

However, it has been largely successful, making it an inspiration for other cryptocurrencies in the market today, such as Ethereum, Litecoin, XRP, Tether, Cardano, and a host of many others.

In this book, we'll be covering what there is to know about Bitcoins and how you can use this knowledge to your benefit. This book is simple enough for beginners yet comprehensive enough for those already in the world of cryptocurrencies.

Chapter 1: What is Bitcoin?

Bitcoin is a digital currency that was created using a system of cryptography. This means that it is a cryptocurrency which can exist only in a digital form unlike conventional currencies (also known as fiat currencies) that can exist in a physical form (like a hundred dollar bill). Cryptocurrencies like Bitcoin, Ethereum, Litecoin, and XRP have a unique characteristic in that they are decentralized. Being decentralized means that no central authority or governing body oversees or controls the network of cryptocurrencies. Everything that works about the Bitcoin is carried out by the public network of users.

The First Digital Currencies

Digital currencies have been around longer than most people think. The history of digital currencies began with the first online money created by an American cryptographer, David Chaum. He created a digital currency in the Netherlands known as DigiCash in the 1990s. DigiCash used an encryption algorithm called the Rivest Shamir Adleman (RSA), which was quite common then. This currency, however, declared bankruptcy in 1998.

Another form of online payment was formed following DigiCash, one that most people are familiar with, PayPal. PayPal allowed merchants to exchange money on the internet; however, they only used currencies that people were already familiar with.

Yet another digital currency that followed was known as E-Gold. This currency had millions of users and operated by issuing credits (called e-gold or gold credits) in exchange for actual gold. E-gold was shut down by the US Government in 2008 due to numerous fraudulent schemes that existed around it.

The Origin of Bitcoin

"The root problem with conventional currencies is all the trust that's required to make it work. The central bank must be trusted not to debase the currency, but the history of fiat currencies is full of breaches of that trust." Satoshi Nakamoto.

Bitcoin was created by the pseudonymous person or group of persons Satoshi Nakamoto with a view of overcoming the challenges of conventional currencies. It was created in 2008, but it wasn't until 2009 that Bitcoin hit the market for use. The first block of Bitcoins was mined on the 3rd of January 2009 by the creator himself. This is known as the genesis block (or block number 0), which gave the miner a reward of 50 Bitcoins. Bitcoin quickly gained recognition and rose in popularity in the early 2010s. By 2014, Bitcoin was being used and accepted as payment for fees, paid at over the counter stores and online purchases such as video games and software. Bitcoin was even accepted as donations on websites such as WikiLeaks.

Why is Satoshi Nakamoto Anonymous?

Bitcoin has caused some controversy in the financial markets, to the extent that they have been banned in certain countries such as Columbia, Ecuador, and Vietnam. Bitcoins are also extremely valuable in the market today. With popularities so high that it's able to trigger government action and value that tempts greed, there are many reasons why the creator(s) of such a currency would want to maintain anonymity.

The ability of Bitcoins to supersede the use of fiat currency is very real and a threat to the governments that issue them. This makes the creator, Satoshi, Nakamoto, a target to rivals. It also stands to reason that the creator of Bitcoin would possess them in reasonable quantities. This could make Satoshi a target for criminals as well. To maintain safety, as well as to avoid unnecessary legal complaints, staying anonymous appears to be the best course of action for Satoshi Nakamoto.

Chapter 2: How Bitcoin Works

Bitcoin is completely digital and operates using cryptography, which is why it's called a cryptocurrency. To be able to use Bitcoins, a user must first obtain a digital wallet, which is used to acquire and trade the cryptocurrency. A digital wallet provides the user with an online address that is unique for each user at the time of creation and transactions. Bitcoin works by using peer to peer technology, which involves a large network of people that exchange information within the Bitcoin network.

The exchange of Bitcoins within this network is done in a framework called a BLOCKCHAIN. The blockchain is a shared public ledger on which the entire Bitcoin network relies. All confirmed transactions are included in the blockchain The exchange of Bitcoins only takes place when two parties agree to a contract. When this transaction takes place between Bitcoin wallets, the data containing information about the sender, the receiving party, and the amount of Bitcoin transferred is entered into the blockchain in chronological order and stored there permanently. The blockchain offers its form of security for the Bitcoin cryptocurrency. Since it's a centralized public record anyone can access, the blockchain offers transparency where people can detect discrepancies. In addition to this, every Bitcoin transaction is done with a pair of keys.

Each user is identified with a pair of keys; the public key and the private key. The keys are mathematical signatures used in cryptography to ascertain that the transactions are carried out by the correct individuals. The private key uses a piece of unique data for each Bitcoin wallet and appends it to the transaction as a form of signature. In contrast, the public key can be used by peers on the Bitcoin network to confirm the validity of the transaction by that specific user at any time. This method provides an extra boost of security for cryptocurrencies because, unlike a written signature and credit card information, the digital signature of a private key cannot be faked or stolen by a scam artist.

Bitcoin eliminates the need for an intermediary or a

third party since all of its transaction records are open to the public for verification. This allows Bitcoins to have a lot of flexibility for use in the market.

So, now we know that Bitcoins use chronological, well-kept, detailed records of transactions in blockchains which can be accessed anytime to prove contracts so no one can take advantage of or cheat the system, but several questions remain:

- What can you do with Bitcoins?

- Where does its value come from? and

- How can I acquire Bitcoins?

We'll be discussing these aspects shortly.

Things Can You Do With Bitcoins

Bitcoins can be used in online stores to pay for goods and services; items can be sold for Bitcoins as well. Bitcoin is extremely versatile and can be used for almost any transaction. Bitcoins also appeals to the masses since it can be used across borders without any restrictions, and it has a fixed value throughout the world. One can view cryptocurrency as a unifying currency. As Bitcoins continue to grow in popularity, so do its possibilities. There are now more things you can do with Bitcoins today than was possible several years ago. Here are just a few of the things you can do with Bitcoins:

Spending

Bitcoin offers a very quick and easy way to pay electronically. This has led to it becoming a common form of payment online and in-store in so many places today. Bitcoins can be spent both locally and internationally on almost anything.

Direct Funding

One of the greatest strengths of Bitcoin is its ability to cut off third-party interference completely. Bitcoins can be used to get funds directly to people in need without having to pay through a platform or organization. This saves a great deal of time since using a third party usually takes time to process your transfer request, especially across borders. Direct funding to people also cuts costs by avoiding extra fees that come with using a third party. A common example of this is using Bitcoins to send charities across the world by areas affected or impacted by disasters. Bitcoins can be used to quickly send relief aids to those in need when they need it.

Sports Betting and Gambling

Bitcoin facilitates wagers and bets without disclosing too much personal information, as is the case with standard betting that requires a credit card and bank information. Bitcoin transactions are fast, secure, and non-refundable, making Bitcoins a great means of betting and gambling online since all that you need are the available funds, no questions asked.

A word of caution: readers are encouraged to ensure that online gambling and sports betting is legal in your location and are advised to gamble responsibly.

Investments

One of the most common uses of Bitcoins is to invest them. Bitcoins can be used to buy gold, silver, and other precious metals. Users can also decide to invest in Bitcoins. Bitcoins have been around for about a decade and has seen rapid growth since its conception; however, there is still plenty of more room for Bitcoins to grow and bring in more users. Investors who see potential in this cryptocurrency's future, as well as many others, can invest in them to benefit financially in the long run.

So basically, Bitcoins can be used in as many ways as we use money today. To better understand the concept of how Bitcoins and other cryptocurrencies are used in the market, let us take a closer look at money.

Understanding Money

"Money is the most universal and most efficient system of mutual trust ever devised." Yuval Harari (Sapiens: A Brief History of Humankind).

To put it simply, money is an agreed-upon medium with an agreed-upon value. When you hold a random hundred dollar bill, and a random one dollar bill side by side in the United States, a majority, if not all, Americans would agree that the hundred dollar bill holds more value than the one-dollar bill. But to a farming village deep in the forest, who've never heard of "dollars," both notes would probably be worthless pieces of paper. The farmers don't agree on what the dollar represents, nor would they use it to trade in the village. To them, a cup of manure has more value than a worthless $100 bill. Over time throughout the history of humankind, money has come in many different forms, shapes, and sizes. From barley to gold and silver coin, even to cowries and shells. What all of these things had in common was that people were willing to exchange them for goods and services among themselves. People kept changing and improving money to overcome certain challenges over again up until the system we have now. Bitcoins and other cryptocurrencies were created to overcome the challenges faced by money under a centralized system of government. This leads us to the next question, what are the various types of money, and how are cryptocurrencies different from other kinds of money?

Characteristics of Money

Money possesses several attributes that extend to Bitcoins and other cryptocurrencies. Example of these attributes include:

1. Scarcity. Money has a limited amount in circulation. By limiting the amount of money, it has worth/value. This is why common everyday objects or materials like sand are not used as money.

2. Divisibility. Money can be easily distributed among people. For example, gold can be melted to make coins and shared among several individuals, unlike say, a statue worth a large amount only as a standing sculpture. Breaking such a statue destroys its value; hence it becomes indivisible, and hence why we can't use art as money.

3. Recognizability and Acceptability. An important characteristic of money is its ability to be easily recognized by its users and accepted among them as means of transaction

4. Durability. Money can be stored for long periods without fear of it losing value. Gold, for example, has been valued by people since time immemorial, unlike shells and cowries, which quickly lost their value.

Types of Money

In the world we live in today, money can be classified into one of two forms; Fiat money and Digital money.

Fiat money derives its origin from the Latin word

fiat, which translates to "by decree." Fiat money is the kind of money that obtains its worth from a higher governing authority recognized by the people. Fiat currency is known as "legal tender" and must be accepted as a means of payment by the citizens of the governing body.

Money that exists as data or code, outside a physical form such as paper money is digital money. Even fiat money can become digital money if its form of transaction takes place online on the internet through sites such as PayPal and online credit card transactions. Cryptocurrencies like Bitcoin, Ethereum, Litecoin, and so on, by their nature, can only ever be a digital money. Digital money has greatly reduced the amount of physical cash in circulation and presented to us a host of benefits, especially in terms of convenience on how transactions are carried out.

Cryptocurrencies vs. Fiat Currency

The major and most important difference between cryptocurrencies and fiat currency is that the former has a decentralized authority, while the latter has a centralized authority. This difference gives cryptocurrencies several advantages over fiat currencies. Among these are:

1. By using a centralized monetary system, you are surrendering all control of your money to the governing agency. Such money is prone to risks of

mismanagements and corruption. For example, the government can decide to print more money and put it in the market without your knowledge or consent. By doing so, there would be excess money in circulation, which would affect the demand and supply, causing the value of yours to go down. Cryptocurrencies can avoid this risk completely. There are no centralized agencies that make decisions about people's money, and all transactions are open and secure in the blockchain public ledgers. Cryptocurrencies also have a limited number of tokens online in circulation, which eliminates the risk of overprinting.

2. Fiat currencies can also have their "legal tender" status revoked by the government. This is also a disadvantage of having a centralized monetary system. Since this money is issued by the government and declared as having worth based on authority, there's also the risk of the government declaring that currency does not have value anymore, making all notes of that currency, even the physical ones, worthless. Once again, cryptocurrencies can avoid this risk. No authority can declare cryptocurrencies worthless. As long as there are people online who are willing to accept a cryptocurrency as a form of payment, it'll always be viewed as money and have worth.

3. In terms of security, cryptocurrencies offer a great deal of security against risks of fraudulent activities. Since they are exclusively digital,

cryptocurrencies cannot be faked. It is impossible to make fake transactions of cryptocurrencies online as well. This is because all records are kept on a single public ledger, the blockchain within the cryptocurrency network. Fiat currencies, on the other hand, can be counterfeited, with the fake notes pushed into circulation by fraudsters. Hackers on the internet can also obtain account and card details to steal fiat currency easily.

Chapter 3: Working with Bitcoins

With millions of users all over the world, Bitcoins are one of the most common currencies in use today. Most stores and businesses have a Bitcoin payment option, and many people are willing to accept as payment too. As at the end of June 2020, there were over 50 million Bitcoin wallets. Since it's so popular, many new users are entering the Bitcoin network as well. Users, therefore, are faced with the challenge of how to get Bitcoins. In this chapter, we'll be looking at the various ways new users can get into the Bitcoin network to begin trading.

When working with Bitcoins, the first thing one has

to do is to obtain a Bitcoin wallet. A Bitcoin wallet stores the information about the user and enables them to send and receive Bitcoins. The wallet contains the public key and the private key, which was discussed earlier.

Where Does the Value of Bitcoin Come From?

Why do people acquire Bitcoins in the first place? Is it really worth it? Well, it's simple to answer these questions. Bitcoin has purchasing power. It can be used to negotiate prices, and its value fluctuates with time just like any other currency. As mentioned earlier, Bitcoins and many other cryptocurrencies such as Litecoin don't have a centralized agency or a regulatory body to determine their value to meet market demands. So, where do cryptocurrencies get their worth?

Bitcoin is currently being used by millions of merchants around the world to process payments for goods and services. In the last chapter, we talked about some of the uses of Bitcoins and how cryptocurrencies can be used as money vis-à-vis fiat currencies. Bitcoin is easily recognizable, it's durable, scarce, and easily transferred from one person to another. Bitcoin is also trusted and accepted within a large network of users. The value of Bitcoin comes from the number of people that are ready to use it as a currency. The more people become aware of Bitcoin and its advantages, the higher the demand for it, which in turn raises its value. Bitcoin also has a limited amount in circulation in the market, which tends to make the value even higher as more people adopt this cryptocurrency. Depending on its demand and supply, the price of Bitcoins fluctuates in the market.

How Can You Acquire Bitcoins?

The major and perhaps most profitable method of acquiring Bitcoins is a process known as mining. Bitcoin does not involve a person carrying a pickaxe and swinging it at a hard rock to find mineral resources. Bitcoin mining is a process that helps the Bitcoin network with the complex mathematical problem to keep the network moving forward. When transactions are carried out, it takes some time to confirm them, usually 10 – 20 minutes. As these mathematical equations are solved, new Bitcoins are generated. Bitcoin mining helps create new Bitcoins to be supplied to the market until the limit/cap of 21 million Bitcoins has been achieved. The people who carry out this process are called miners. Bitcoin miners are the ones who make it possible for new Bitcoins to be brought into circulation. In addition to generating new Bitcoins to be supplied to the market, Bitcoin miners also allow the blockchain to move forward by confirming transactions in chronological order. For new transactions to follow through in the Bitcoin network, previous transactions need to be confirmed. This is extremely important to keep the Bitcoin network up and running.

Since miners are so essential to the smooth running of the Bitcoin network, there is a reward system in place for the people who help in providing the computational power due to the intensive electrical power required to run the mathematical process in Bitcoin transactions. Miners also come together to share resources and improve the efficiency of mining in what are known as mining pools. Of course, mining pools have to share the rewards for mining each block of Bitcoins among themselves, but the amount earned and the cut in costs is enough to make the participants in a mining pool stay motivated. For each new block that is mined, miners receive newly created Bitcoin as compensation in addition to a small tip. This reward was 50 Bitcoins at first, which is halved after every 210,000 Bitcoin is mined roughly every 4 years. This means the reward has been reduced from 50 to 25, and is now at 12.5 Bitcoins per block mined.

Bitcoin Mining Tools

Mining Bitcoins is a resource-intensive task that gets harder as more blocks as mined. To compensate for the high energy demand used in solving the SHA-256 algorithm, people have created tools and devices dedicated to solving these problems and mining the Bitcoins. Mining dedicated hardware has seen transformations throughout the history of Bitcoin to improve efficiency. However, most Bitcoin mining hardware is very expensive and consumes a large amount of electricity. To make a good profit using these dedicated mining tools, users must first calculate the electricity consumption fees required to run the hardware, as well as maintenance fees. So, after considering the resources required, here are some of the hardware used, specifically for mining Bitcoins and how they have changed with time:

Central Processing Unit (CPU)

When Bitcoin launched in 2009, all it took was a CPU to compute the algorithms for mining the blocks. There was very little competition on the market, and so all users needed for mining Bitcoins was the CPU in their computers or laptops.

Graphics Processing Unit (GPU)

This is a piece of hardware that is dedicated to rendering graphics on a computer. Bitcoin miners quickly realized that GPUs were much faster and more efficient in calculating the algorithms for blockchains. Many miners switched from CPUs to GPUs, causing an amazing increase in the strength and productivity of the Bitcoin network.

Field Programming Gate Array (FPGA)

Even though GPUs were very effective for a while,

the nature of blockchains made mathematical computations more complex as more people joined the network. Only computers and laptops with powerful inbuilt CPUs and GPUs, which consumed a lot of power, were being used to mine Bitcoins. This all changed when gate arrays hit the markets. FPGAs are integrated circuits (IC) that can easily be configured once purchased. FPGA was more powerful than GPUs and consumed less energy as well.

Application Specific Integrated Circuit (ASIC)

Bitcoin miners realized that they need to keep making better hardware to keep up with the higher demand for computational power required to run the Bitcoin network. So the hardware for Bitcoin mining kept on evolving and improving. There was yet to be a piece of hardware whose sole purpose was just for Bitcoin mining. ASIC was made specifically for Bitcoin mining in the year 2013, and they were even better and more energy-efficient that all the other hardware that came before it. Although ASICs were faster and consumed less energy, there were some downsides to owning them. ASICs generated high amounts of heat while running, and they are very loud as well. Also, not all Bitcoin miners can afford one. ASICs are quite expensive in addition to being very heavy, which amounts to significant shipping and taxation costs. Last but not least, ASICs have a limited lifespan, usually about 1.5 Terrahash, before they are no longer functional. All of the downsides of ASICs should be weighed with the user's financial capabilities before considering using it to go into the Bitcoin mining business.

Bitcoin Mining Software

There are several software that can aid users in mining Bitcoins more efficiently. Bitcoin mining software is usually free and can be just as important as the hardware. Mining software helps miners link up to the Bitcoin network as well as connect to a pool of other miners. The software helps record the computed work of the hardware and puts it in the Bitcoin network. In addition to this, it is also regularly updated on the status of other miners' blockchains on the Bitcoin network. Some software to aid mining Bitcoin include:

CGMiner

This software is popular in the Bitcoin mining community and arguably one of the best. It has advanced features such as being able to detect and start mining blocks on its own. In addition to being able to run on older hardware like GPU, CGMiner also runs on all major operating system platforms like Windows, Linux, and Mac.

EasyMiner

This uses a Graphical User Interface (GUI), which

makes it easier for miners to visualize and control the mining process. It has the added advantage of being able to mine not just Bitcoin, but other cryptocurrencies like Litecoin as well. However, a limitation to EasyMiner is that it's available only on the Windows platform and operates using only the ASIC hardware.

BitMiner

This software also uses a GUI like EasyMiner, but with the added benefit of being able to run on all major platforms like Windows, Linux, and Mac, and with the GPU, FPGA, and ASIC hardware. This software also adds you to a mining pool that's hundreds of thousands strong, making it an option with good returns.

MultiMiner

A major strength of this software is how easily it allows miners to mine different kinds of cryptocurrencies and not just Bitcoin. MultiMiner is also GUI based and works on all major operating system platforms. It hosts a wide array of options like displaying miners' hardware details, including specs, temperature, and so on. It can also be automated to mine the cryptocurrency with the "highest potential for profit."

Other Ways to Acquire More Bitcoins

Besides mining, there are other ways one can go about getting more Bitcoins.

Buying Bitcoins

This is the most direct and straightforward method of acquiring Bitcoins, but it's also the only method that comes at a financial cost. Buying Bitcoins involves exchanging physical cash or fiat currencies for cryptocurrencies. To do this, the buyer must find a platform that they can use for the exchange of fiat currencies for cryptocurrencies. Such exchanges are popularly known as foreign exchange or FOREX for short.

Compared to obtaining a Bitcoin wallet, which is relatively easy, finding the right platform to exchange cash for cryptocurrencies poses challenges of its own. Even though Bitcoin is borderless, there might be some legal challenges in some governments that don't recognize Bitcoins. This may make it difficult to convert Bitcoins to the local currency if the user intends to withdraw funds. Finding the right platform is also important. Different platforms charge at different rates when conducting exchanges, while other platforms take small percentages of funds from every transaction made on their site. There's also the risk of fraudulent websites which pose as foreign exchange sites. One of the main reasons why Bitcoin was created is to remove the need for a middleman and give users complete control of their money. However, since registering on platforms involves entering user information such as name, phone number, address, and other bank details, you are deciding to trust your funds as well as your anonymity to a third party. It is, therefore, extremely important that users do adequate research before choosing to trust any FOREX platform.

Getting Paid

One of the easiest ways to acquire Bitcoins is to earn it through the goods and services rendered. People with Bitcoin wallets can choose to get paid in Bitcoins upon completion of tasks. However, before embarking on such a task, as a user, you must ensure that your client is willing to pay the agreed amount in cryptocurrencies and has the means to allocate you your funds once the contract is fulfilled.

Forums

Several online forums provide users with the opportunity to earn Bitcoins as rewards and tips for staying active on the forum. These sites are popular among many businesses and get a huge amount of views and following. To encourage more visits to the site and generate income, forum users are rewarded as an incentive. Each user has a forum signature that is used to keep track of user activity. The rewards vary depending on the extent to which the user is active on the platform. Users who make insightful posts are rewarded higher than those who don't. Also, the posts on sight have to be constructive and not be repetitive. By spamming the site, users risk getting kicked off the platform and losing their account.

Faucets

One of the easiest and most passive methods of acquiring Bitcoins is through faucets. Simply by visiting certain websites during certain periods, users get rewarded with Bitcoins. Faucets can pay Bitcoins to people who visit their sites based on ad revenues. To attract potential customers, companies pay faucet websites to host their banners. In turn, they share some of that revenue to people who visit their sites to garner more visibility. It is important to note, however, that faucets pay very little, and more often than not, this method takes a lot of time. Users shouldn't think of getting rich quickly with this method.

Affiliate Marketing

Bitcoin affiliates offer you rewards in Bitcoins by providing affiliate links on your own platform like a blog or YouTube channel. Affiliate marketing requires you to have some form of social media presence that you can then use to bring in potential customers by sharing a unique link on your platform. When the potential customer clicks the link, it directs them to the company's site, and when they make a purchase, you get rewarded.

Cloud Mining

This method is an innovative way of mining Bitcoins, but instead of using your own hardware, you are using another user's hardware. Cloud mining allows users to acquire Bitcoins directly in exchange for fees in which you pay the sites hosting the hardware. This method is convenient and allows users to overcome the obstacle posed by having to own hardware for Bitcoin mining. Cloud mining also removes the need for having to secure the high demand of electric power required to run the Bitcoin mining hardware. Users also save time and shipping costs by using cloud mining and VAT issues are completely avoided as well. Cloud mining is also quick and puts the user in a mining pool without them having to go through too many technicalities and gives additional advantages than mining as an individual.

When it comes to the downside of cloud mining, the most obvious risk is having to put your trust entirely in a third-party. Cloud mining doesn't give a user any control of the Bitcoins mined, nor does it give access to the hardware itself. The Bitcoins a user receives from cloud mining lie completely at the discretion of the miner offering the services. There is not enough transparency in cloud mining. The owner of the hardware may or may not have legitimate reasons for charging extra fees or for allocating fewer Bitcoins to cover the expenses of hosting the hardware. Another major risk when it comes to cloud mining is legitimacy. You stand a risk of paying fees to fraudulent websites that pretend to offer cloud mining services often with pictures. Users, therefore, have the responsibility of doing extensive research to determine whether or not they can trust the host. One more disadvantage of cloud mining is that since they are usually a mining pool with public information offering their services, cloud mining services are usually the target of hackers. Being a target puts your funds at risk. If they do get hacked, all users of the service are negatively impacted by the losses.

Chapter 4: The Future of Cryptocurrencies: Should You Invest in Bitcoins?

Bitcoins, along with many other cryptocurrencies, is rapidly gaining momentum among users. The world is quickly becoming a global market, and online transactions are becoming the norm. Merchants across the globe need a way to quickly send payments securely, at low costs, and in a currency that the buyer recognizes. Cryptocurrencies solve all of these problems while giving users absolute control over their finances without the involvement of a third party.

Most people are instantly wowed whenever they hear the current value of Bitcoins in comparison to its previous value in the past. The increase in value is astonishing, and so some begin to wonder if they should start investing in Bitcoins, while others are immediately tempted to buy some. What these people fail to realize is the time it took for Bitcoins to reach its current value. Even though Bitcoin is a durable currency, its immediate value over short periods is not stable. For those who don't know what they are doing, trying to time the market to make quick bucks off of Bitcoin is an extremely bad idea. Digital currencies have been growing, and in the long foreseeable future, will continue to do so. In fact, there is still a lot of untapped potential for cryptocurrencies, especially in places like Africa and Asia, where digital currencies have not been fully adopted. It is therefore recommended that new investors approach Bitcoins with a long term view rather than a short term one.

In this chapter, we'll be discussing whether or not it's a good idea to invest your time and money in acquiring Bitcoins if you can trust Bitcoins and other cryptocurrencies, the risks involved in them as well as their advantages and disadvantages.

Can You Trust Bitcoins?

One of the biggest hurdles every new idea has to overcome is the issue of trust. When Bitcoins hit the markets, it didn't immediately become the number one cryptocurrency on the market. It had to prove itself as something people can trust. A reliable alternative as it claimed to be. To this day, many people have their misgivings about Bitcoins and cryptocurrencies in general. One of the biggest trust issues facing Bitcoin is that it's a decentralized currency, and due to this, no agency can assure you that your funds are insured. Once your funds are lost or stolen, they are gone forever with no chance of recovery. The decentralized nature of Bitcoin also means that it depends on its users to keep it running. Every Bitcoin wallet is an essential part of the Bitcoin wallet since there's no central authority or figure to regulate the network. However, this can be viewed as a strength of Bitcoin and not a weakness. This is because, for the Bitcoin network to collapse, it'll involve over 50 million users to agree that they no longer want to use Bitcoins as a currency. This seems nearly impossible and, therefore, highly unlikely to happen.

To be able to trust Bitcoins, it's important that you better understand it. Doing so will help ease security concerns about the cryptocurrency. We've already discussed in an earlier chapter how Bitcoin technology works using blockchains and peer to peer networks. Security concerns about funds getting stolen are few. Getting people to put their faith in cryptocurrency, however, is the bigger challenge.

Critics of cryptocurrencies have always condemned Bitcoin as "not being real money." Still, such talk should be expected, especially since cryptocurrencies are new players in the market challenging the status quo. For those who want more control of their finances without much interference from the government or banks, the idea of cryptocurrencies is very alluring. When millions of users exchange Bitcoins on the internet, they do so without any extra fees from banks, nor do they have to worry about conversion rates. Bitcoin offers not just security but complete financial freedom to its users. A lot of people have understood this, and as more and more understand this concept, Bitcoin actually gets stronger in the market. It has become heavily integrated into many financial systems and is widely accepted side by side fiat currencies, with the added benefit of fewer fees, more control, and fewer infrastructures. In short, you can trust Bitcoins because it works; it has a proven track record and is accepted by millions.

The Risks of Investing Bitcoins

Like they say, "the highest returns usually involve the highest risks." Although Bitcoin has seen a significant rise in the market, first in 2011, then in 2013 and in 2017, when it reached its all-time high so far, Bitcoin isn't without its risks. Many investors are drawn to Bitcoin for its future potential more so than its use as a currency for buying and selling. Again, it is important to remember that Bitcoin is not centralized under the government or any supervising authority. This makes the currency prone to several risks. Also, unlike fiat currencies, Bitcoins have been around for only about a decade, making it relatively young in the world of finances.

Cryptocurrencies are still, for the most part, experimental and developing. There is still a lot of progress to be made before Bitcoin can become stable. To make reasonable investments in Bitcoins or any other cryptocurrencies, investors must exercise due caution. Here are some things investors should look out for before investing in Bitcoin:

Insurance Risk

In some cases, bank firms or other brokerage firms might experience bankruptcy or loss of assets. Several organizations provide insurance against such unforeseen circumstances. Organizations like the Securities Investor Protection Corporation (SPIC) and the Federal Deposit Insurance Corporation (FDIC) help investors protect their stocks and other investments. Such securities cannot be enjoyed by people who invest in Bitcoin. When investors go into Bitcoin investment, they should be well aware that their funds are not backed or guaranteed for by any agency.

Tax Risk

This occurs when taxation rules are changed, leading to an unexpected rise in taxes, resulting in losses. Bitcoins do not qualify for a taxed advantaged retirement account, which makes Bitcoin investments vulnerable to taxations.

Scams

Bitcoin has been used for numerous scams by fraudsters on the internet. One example of this is when false Bitcoins are sold on the internet by fraudsters in exchange for real money. Another example is an exit scam, where investors are gathered on a new platform by internet crooks to gather Bitcoins from investors before disappearing with no trace. Unfortunately, the cryptographic nature of Bitcoins makes it difficult to trace the scammers. One last example exists in the form of Multi-Level Marketing Systems. These systems promise users high returns based heavily on the number of additional users they can recruit, but not before collecting some funds first. By collecting funds from investors, they give them tokens, which they are forced to convince other potential customers to buy off their hands. Multi-Level Marketing Systems promise rewards to old investors only if they can bring in new investors. When this inflow of new investors stop coming in, the ones at the top usually pack up and leave, leaving those who have invested at the bottom with nothing. To avoid scams, investors can take the following precautions:

1. Certify the credibility of the platform before investing. Many exit scams have fake credentials which they buy off random internet sites. Setting up a team for handling cryptocurrencies is very expensive,

and investors can ask for the track record of sponsors to ensure that they are legit before venturing into the platform.

2. Consider their projected returns before investing. If the returns being promised by an ICO is realistic, then an investor can assume they are practical about their investments. However, ICOs with a ridiculously huge amount of returns in short periods are just looking to gather investors' funds. Avoid such platforms. An unfortunate example of this can be seen in the case with BitConnect, which turned out to be a Ponzi scheme that shut down in January 2018. BitConnect promised users up to five thousand percent (5000%) returns in three years. This unrealistic goal was met with overeager investors, making BitConnect market cap rise to $2.7 billion by December 2017, but worth a measly $17 million in comparison by the time they closed down, devastating the funds of many investors.

3. Make sure they have a working model that clearly spells out how the platform operates. Investors have a responsibility to understand at least to an extent how a platform intends to operate using their funds. If the ICOs don't have a working model to follow, it becomes clear that they

just want to convince investors so they can run off eventually with funds.

Risk of Regulation

Bitcoin is an open challenge that aims to rival government currencies. The nature of cryptocurrencies makes them easy to be used for several activities that might warrant government attention. Those activities include tax evasion, illegal cross border and black-market payments, money laundering, and the emergence of a high number of schemes and frauds that aim to swindle honest investors. This can make government authorities crackdown on the use of cryptocurrencies at any moment's notice. An example of such an event happened in the People's Republic of China. The Chinese government banned the use of Initial Coin Offerings (ICOs) in September 2017 and ordered all platforms are trading ICOs to shut down. South Korea is another example of a country where ICOs have been banned. Government involvement in Bitcoins in the form of regulation and control measures go against the core values of Bitcoin. However, since the government has the power to make Bitcoins illegal, there is a risk to the longevity and universal acceptance of the currency.

Market Risk

Bitcoin's value is not set in stone. Like any other currency, Bitcoin's value changes in the market.

Bitcoin can be very volatile, with an example of its price margins varying as high as 80% in just a single day. As mentioned earlier, all of Bitcoin's worth lies in the number of people who are willing to accept it as a currency. Although Bitcoin is the most successful among all of the cryptocurrencies, with the longest and most successful track record, investors risk people moving over to a newer and more innovative cryptocurrency. This would cause Bitcoins to lose a great deal of value, or in the worst-case scenario, become almost worthless in the market.

Chapter 5: The Advantages and Disadvantages of Bitcoins

There are many reasons why Bitcoin is the most popular cryptocurrency today. Bitcoins are an amazing alternative to conventional currencies, and in addition to this, they open up a host of possibilities in the financial market. Bitcoin also has its shortcomings; which users should be aware of. In this final chapter, we'll be looking at some of the pros and cons of owning Bitcoins. A lot of these opinions are entirely subjective. They may or may not hold true for everyone.

Advantages of Bitcoin

We'll start by looking at some of the strengths of Bitcoins and why it's a better form of currency than fiat currencies.

Control

This is one of the greatest strengths of Bitcoin. Bitcoin offers its users absolute control over their finances. Users no longer depend on infrastructure created by someone else, but rather the peer to peer technology they have complete control over. There are no spending limits, no transaction fees, and no limitations whatsoever on what you can do with your funds. This financial freedom offers users of Bitcoins far more convenience than credit or debit cards.

For many people, it doesn't make sense for banks or governments to hold their finances, to tell them how or when they can spend their money. It doesn't make sense to be charged for spending either. Bitcoin puts the power of control in the hands of the people so they can't be duped into over-relying on governments.

Transparency

Bitcoins operate in an open network with a public ledger using peer to peer technology. Bitcoin allows anyone to track and verify payments on the blockchain public ledger, making transactions quick and hassle-free.

Privacy

Bitcoin grants anonymity to its users when they perform their transactions. Users can easily spend and transfer funds without having to give away their personal information or provide verification, which is a requirement when using banks or other platforms such as Western Union or MoneyGram.

Borderless Transactions with No Fees

One of the more alluring aspects of Bitcoins is that there is no extra charge for sending money across borders. Almost all fiat currency platforms today charge a substantial amount of money to send payments depending on the location and amount of money sent. There are also a limited number of ways one can do this, take for example, if the receiving party can only accept funds through Western Union, but the nearest branch that offers that service is far away from you. Bitcoin allows merchants to transfer funds across borders all too easy at no extra charges.

Higher Level of Security

Bitcoins cannot be manipulated or controlled by bankers or government officials who can decide the value of a currency to control the market. The decentralized nature of Bitcoin protects the currency and user's funds from being easily manipulated. Instead, it is only the market's demand and supply that truly determines the value of Bitcoins. In addition to this, blockchain technology provides high levels of protection to users' finances, making it almost impossible for cryptocurrencies to be stolen from a user's wallet. The blockchain technology is also being continually improved and upgraded, so Bitcoin also provides security in terms of future prospects of the cryptocurrency.

Speed

Bitcoin transactions do not have to wait for confirmation from a third party to be carried out. Merchants across the world can receive and confirm payments very quickly with Bitcoins, allowing them to act quickly and deliver goods and services. Financial disagreements that may occur among traders online usually take even longer to be resolved by banks and credit card companies. Issuing refunds and chargebacks are a slow grueling process that slows down business. However, this can also be quickly resolved using Bitcoins. All that is needed is an agreement between traders to transfer funds to the paying address in the event of a refund.

Originality

Thanks to blockchain technology, there is no risk of fake Bitcoins existing in the market. Bitcoin cannot have counterfeit copies, unlike fiat currencies.

Welcoming

Bitcoin strives on the number of users that are willing to accept it as a currency, and as such, there is little to no barrier to entering the Bitcoin network. Since Bitcoins are highly divisible up to a unit of 0.0000001 BTC (known as a Satoshi), it has become very easy for anyone with any level of financial capability to start acquiring Bitcoins.

Autonomous

Bitcoins are independent of other currencies in the market, having its value strictly dictated by its terms. Bitcoins are very similar to gold and silver in this regard. Government law and policies have very little impact on the actual value of Bitcoins in the market.

Limited Quantity

Bitcoins have a limited amount in circulation in the market, making it deflationary in the long run. Only 21 million Bitcoins can be mined and put into the market. By placing such a cap on Bitcoin, it behaves just like limited resources (gold, for example), causing its value to increase due to its limited supply.

Disadvantages of Bitcoin

Now that we've discussed some of the pros of Bitcoins, it's time we consider the other side of this coin (pun intended). Right off the bat, all of the risks of Bitcoins discussed in Chapter four apply here, so we will not be discussing those aspects any further than necessary here. With that being said, here are some of the challenges facing Bitcoin today:

Lack of Awareness

The success of Bitcoin relies heavily on people knowing about it and using it for their daily activities. However, Bitcoin is relatively a young child in the market compared to fiat currencies. People tend to stick to the things they already know and are comfortable with. This makes it difficult to sell the idea of Bitcoin to people. The numerous scams carried out in the name of Bitcoin has also done nothing to help this situation. Bad news like that tends to travel faster and wider than the success stories of Bitcoins, which hinders the progress of the cryptocurrencies even more. Since the strength of Bitcoins lies in how many people use the currency, it becomes, therefore, the responsibility of the current users to educate and bring awareness about Bitcoin to the public.

Complicated

You don't need to take anyone to school to teach them how to spend a dollar. Conventional money is very easy to understand and use. Bitcoins, however, have a complex and complicated mechanism that not everyone will understand. Even the people spending Bitcoins today may not know exactly how blockchains work, all they do is use Bitcoin simply as a digital currency. The technical aspects of Bitcoin have turned away many would-be users when, in reality, it's not really important to know every single aspect of it. Users of this cryptocurrency can aid this situation by focusing on the important aspects of Bitcoin, such as security and practicality.

Limited Use

Since not everyone has accepted Bitcoins, there will be some limitations in how and where they can be used. Many places price goods and services in dollars and other common fiat currencies before converting them to Bitcoins (BTC). Also, using Bitcoins to pay bills is usually done with the aid of a platform or middleman, which negates the point of Bitcoin. To make Bitcoin a mainstream currency, intense efforts have to be made to educate people on how to use the cryptocurrency.

Volatility

Bitcoins are very volatile, with its prices swaying by very large amounts in very little time. This property makes it risky to trade, especially in short terms, and turns away potential users.

Irreversible Transactions

This is one of the biggest disadvantages of using

Bitcoins. Once a transaction has been carried out, there is absolutely no way to reverse it; therefore, there is no option of refunds in the Bitcoin network. This lack of safety net for users can be a problem when transactions are critical.

So far, in this chapter, we've looked at and discussed some of the merits of Bitcoins. We looked at the challenges facing the cryptocurrency on its journey to be a widely accepted form of money. We've also seen that the benefits of Bitcoin outweigh the downsides. However, as with everything else in life, nothing is permanent. Things may change at any moment, and investors are advised to use discretion and do some extra research before deciding to go into Bitcoin or any other cryptocurrency.

Since Bitcoins are not the only cryptocurrencies in play on the financial market, what are some other great cryptocurrencies out there that users can look into and buy?

Other Cryptocurrencies

Many other cryptocurrencies have tried to achieve the success that Bitcoin has, and because of this we have a wide array of cryptocurrencies to choose from. Some of these have tried and failed, some are exit scams, while some still are legit, and are making strides on the financial market. For those people who missed catching the big wave of

Bitcoins when it was still young, here are other cryptocurrencies for you to consider that are making their way to prominence on the market.

Ethereum (ETH)

Created by Vitalik Buterin, the idea of this cryptocurrency came onto the scene in 2013. Like many others, Ethereum was inspired by Bitcoin selling over 50 million tokens within the first two weeks of its ICO in 2014. It launched a year later in 2015 and is currently the second biggest cryptocurrency after Bitcoin in terms of market cap with over $15 billion.

Ethereum provides a platform for developers using decentralized blockchain technology to enable the developers to build other blockchain applications called DApp (decentralized apps). Ethereum (or Ethers) operate by using tokens awarded to developers to operate on the platform to create decentralized blockchain technology, or by investors who wish to use it to purchase other cryptocurrencies. Ethereum is supported by a large number of investors, as well as technological giants. This gives Ethereum an edge in terms of development and innovation, crucial aspects of the cryptocurrency market. As at the time of writing this paper in July 2020, a single Ether is worth $395, which is significantly higher, considering it was worth around $142 six months prior.

Ripple (XRP)

Unlike many other cryptocurrencies, ripple does not use blockchain technology. Instead, it uses a distribution of ledgers called the consensus ledger, which is used to confirm transactions. XRPs can be used to confirm international transactions at a very fast rate, with little to no costs. The Ripple XRP cryptocurrency was created by Ripple Labs and is still being maintained by the same organization. Unlike Bitcoin, it uses "pre-mined tokens," which are then distributed to users at a cost. In other words, XRP tokens cannot be mined, only acquired once they are available in the market based on strict guidelines set by the network. This gives Ripple XRPs certain advantages over Bitcoin, such as in terms of computational power required and energy consumption.

Litecoin (LTC)

In the media, Litecoin is popularly referred to as the "silver to Bitcoin's gold." This is because Litecoin has followed Bitcoin's footsteps closely. Created by a graduate of the Massachusetts Institute of Technology (MIT), Charlie Lee, and launched in 2011, Litecoins also uses decentralized blockchain technology and has seen high levels of success. However, unlike Bitcoins, which use an SHA-256 algorithm for its mathematical computations, Litecoins use a Scrypt for its own. The Litecoin algorithm usually takes about 5 minutes to solve, which is half the time it takes to solve Bitcoin blockchains. Since the computations were relatively easier, many miners were able to keep mining for Litecoins using older hardware that couldn't mine Bitcoins just as efficiently.

Tether (USDT)

To avoid the risks posed by the volatility of Bitcoin and other cryptocurrencies, the idea of tying the value of a cryptocurrency to a fiat currency was born. Tether hit the markets in 2014 and has been able to attract otherwise skeptical investors by reducing and controlling wild fluctuations that are experienced by other cryptocurrencies such as Bitcoin. To put it simply, Tether USDTs are like fiat currency using the blockchain technology of cryptocurrencies. It aims to combine the best of both sides by using the stability of fiat money and adding it to the transparency and security of cryptocurrencies.

Monero (XMR)

In April 2014, Monero was launched and gathered a great deal of interest due to its high levels of anonymity. This decentralized cryptocurrency is untraceable because it uses an innovative method called a ring signature. Ring signatures take a set of cryptographic signatures, at least one of which belongs to the transaction owner, making it difficult to identify the real owner of the transaction since it is amid other signatures which look legit.

EOS (EOS)

At the time of the writing, this cryptocurrency is only 2 years old, making it the youngest on the market in our list. But don't let that fool you, however, because EOS is a strong contender among the older currencies out there. Designed by Dan Larimer, EOS follows in the footsteps of Ethereum, and just like Ripple XRDs, there is no mining on the EOS platform to generate tokens. EOS tokens are earned by users who generate blocks instead. The more blocks generated, the higher the reward, although a set of strict rules also governs this system.

Libra (LIBRA)

The last cryptocurrency on our list is one that, at the time of this writing, has not been launched onto the market. Libra is a digital currency that was pioneered by the giant social media Facebook. The currency was formally announced to the public in June 2019 and is set to be released in 2020. Given the popularity and huge following of Facebook, this cryptocurrency is anticipated to be one of the biggest to be on the financial market after launch.

Conclusion

Bitcoin ushered in a new era of financing that we never thought was possible before. Its open-source nature allowed it to be accessible by all and not just the upper class of society, giving everyone an equal opportunity on the market. It provides a transparent, secure, and very quick means of sending funds for payment of goods and services all over the world without the interference of a third party, unlike conventional money.

Many people have made millions with Bitcoin, and many more will come in the future. Companies and businesses of all sizes and individuals from all walks of life are in this large global network of cryptocurrency, and it still continues to grow. That's why in this book, we've looked at what makes it so successful and how we can approach Bitcoin and cryptocurrencies as a whole with a good level of understanding. We've looked at how strong and secure the network is, the room for growth and potential within the network, strengths, and weaknesses, and how to get started with mining, acquiring and trading Bitcoin. Adequate attention was also given on how to detect and avoid internet fraudsters, who wish to take advantage of honest people new to Bitcoin and any other cryptocurrency for that matter. Always remember to do adequate research on platforms before venturing into investments, and never take risks you cannot afford to lose.

I hope with the help of this book that you are well equipped for your journey into the exciting world of cryptocurrencies.

www.ingramcontent.com/pod-product-compliance
Lightning Source LLC
Chambersburg PA
CBHW060914130726
48001CB00006B/2226